Fearless Little Me

Written By: Khloe Clemons

.

Fearless

Little Me

Written By

Khloe Clemons

Ordering Information:

Quantity sales: Special discounts are available on quantity purchases by corporations, associations, and others. For details, contact the publisher at the address above.

Published by KLC Publishing

Printed in the United States of America

My mommy and daddy told me a secret, and it is as true as can be.

They said I could be anything I wanted. Because I am Fearless little me

I could captain a big, big boat,
and sail the big blue sea!

Because I could be anything
I wanted,
I'm fearless little me!

I could explore the stars and space, defying gravity.

An astronaut could be
in my future,
because I'm fearless little me.

I could win an Olympic Medal, and be the best gymnast you've ever seen!

I would flip and wow, and flip and stretch, because I'm fearless little me.

I could be as brave as a fireman, and work until I made all the fire leave.

Saving lives could be my prize,
because I'm fearless little me.

No matter what I decide to be,
the choice is up to me!

A lawyer, a doctor, a vet fixing pets.

A nurse, a chef, a pilot flying jets

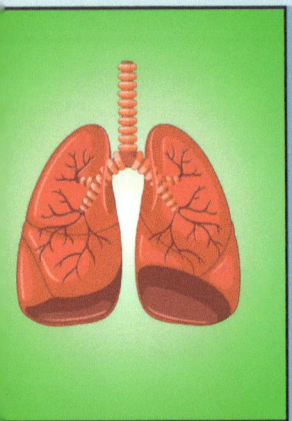

I'll do it fearlessly!
Because fear can not
hold me back,
I'm fearless little me.

Thinking Cap Time!

- What did mommy and daddy tell Khloe?

- What do you want to be when you grow up?

- Why do you want to be this?

- What makes you fearless?

- Name two things Khloe said she could be when she grows up?

The End

Start Your Story

_____

_____

_____

_____

_____

_____

_____

_____

_____

_____

_____

www.ingramcontent.com/pod-product-compliance
Lightning Source LLC
Chambersburg PA
CBHW041819040426
42452CB00001B/24